Joyc Hated Noise

by Claire Daniel
illustrated by Chuck Gonzales

Scott Foresman

Editorial Offices: Glenview, Illinois • New York, New York
Sales Offices: Reading, Massachusetts • Duluth, Georgia
Glenview, Illinois • Carrollton, Texas • Menlo Park, California

Not long ago, there was a princess named Joyce who hated noise. Every morning it was so noisy, she had no choice but to wake up.

"There is too much noise!" Princess Joyce cried.

The rooster crowed. Two noisy boys, Roy and Troy, ran into her room on their way to play.

"Noise even spoils the sunrise!" Joyce cried.

She got up and went to see her father the king about it.

"Father!" she said. "This kingdom is too noisy. Wouldn't it be wonderful without noise?"

"It would be peaceful," her father said. "But I can't do anything about noise. A little noise is not harmful."

"But, Father, this is important!" she said. "Very important!"

"Not now, Joyce," he said. "I have to work. And you need to take Floyd the royal dog out for a walk. Now be careful."

Joyce took Floyd out for a walk. On her way out, she walked by a man counting stacks of gold coins.

"Plop, plop, clink, clink!" The coins made so much noise.

"You're too noisy!" Joyce told the man. But the man did not stop counting.

She walked by Roy and Troy who were playing with their toys.

"You're too noisy, boys!" she told them. But Roy and Troy did not stop playing.

Joyce walked by two men who were lifting a huge piano.

"Heave, ho!" they shouted.

"You're making too much noise!" Joyce cried.

But the men kept working. They shouted over her voice.

Then Floyd saw a cat. Floyd broke free and chased the cat. The cat ran toward the chickens. They began to make a lot of noise.

The chickens flew on top of a mule.
The noisy chickens scared the mule.
The mule kicked over a cart full of
corn. A sack of corn landed on top of
the princess.

Princess Joyce had corn in her crown. She had corn on her dress. She had corn in her mouth. She had corn in her ears.

"Are you all right?" everyone asked.

Princess Joyce did not hear the people. She stood up. She stepped away from the corn. Then she picked up Floyd's leash and headed home.

Princess Joyce could not hear the men lifting the piano. She could not hear the man counting his coins. She could not hear Roy and Troy and their toys.

Princess Joyce could not hear a thing! She was joyful!

Princess Joyce rushed in to see her father. She wanted to share the good news with him. There was no more noise in the kingdom!

Her father did not understand. He heard noise. He tried to talk to her. But she couldn't hear him.

Days passed. Every day was the same. Nothing was different. The rooster crowed. Joyce could not hear it. Roy and Troy ran and played. Joyce did not hear them.

Princess Joyce was unhappy. She couldn't even enjoy the sunrise that filled her room each morning.

"Father," Joyce said, "I think a little noise would be okay. I don't like it when there is no noise."

"Joyce," her father said.

Joyce cried, "I can't hear you!"

Then Joyce shook her head. Corn fell out of her ears. Floyd barked as the corn hit the floor.

"What a wonderful sound!" Joyce said.

Joyce laughed. She enjoyed the different noises her voice made.

Troy and Roy asked her to join them in a race. Joyce said yes. She knew they would let her make a lot of noise.

Honk

Plink

To this day, Joyce lives in a very noisy kingdom. And she likes it that way!